Illuminating HerStory

A safe space to reflect, rebuild, and reclaim your birth story.

Arianna Alloway

DEDICATION

To all the swollen wombs, boobs, hearts and eyes that may dance across these next pages. For the strength and bravery that it takes to walk the adventure of healing your story–and in turn, our Daughters and Granddaughters–Thank you!

A special thanks to my dearest friend, Brittney. Forever thankful for your kindness, encouragement, inspiration, and support. Thank you for being the friend every woman deserves but doesn't always have. xxx

CONTENTS

MAMAMADE SHOUT-OUTS

TheRenegadeMama.com
Affirmation cards and support

for pregnancy, postpartum, and family.

FreeBirthSociety.com
Community, support, and education for women collectively.

Mamamalas.com
Mala beads and accessories that celebrate motherhood and connect you

to what matters.

Bluemoonholistics.bigcartel.com
Honest, natural, intentional handmade teething and beyond jewelry for

mother and babe.

Alohaandlight.com
Beautiful newborn and toddler ring slings hand painted by the sea.

Janaroemer.com
"Yoga Nigra is a practice that ever so gently peels away the layers of

illusion until all that's left is the most innocent, connected part of

yourself that you've been longing to know intimately. When you meet

yourself there, it all starts to make sense. You have to access insights,

inner vision, subconscious programming and self-love."

Transmuting the trauma

into stories helps to evolve

the experience into the

medicine that eventually

restores our trust.

Hello beloved Sister, I am happy that you are here. Congratulations in choosing to step further into your healing, seek support, fully embrace and engage as you journey through this transition.

Whether it has been just weeks since your birth, years, or you are now welcoming another child; the following practices have been created with love and effort to offer guidance and help hold you through your healing.

This book was created throughout my own healing with a wish to support any individual that may be feeling trauma or heaviness from a birthing experience. Perhaps a birth that's not even your own! Although written to the mother, this space is intended for any mother, partner, birth worker, healer or friend that feels a pull to explore a birth experience with more depth. Even the most beautiful and peaceful journey through birth can benefit from reflection and processing.

Birth often leaves us feeling empowered, riding high, and in complete awe of ourselves and the experience. It can also leave us feeling raw, painfully baffled and vulnerable.

Offering a Mother the opportunity to flex her voice, have her story held and witnessed, and to feel heard without judgement is important and necessary. The positive connections help to create or recreate her story. That's not to say this rebirth of her experience is fictional-so far from it. The story sharing can offer the mother tools and space to be able to tell her tale without the gaps, or missing pieces that previously felt too jagged for her to carry alone. Birth story debriefing can assist the mother in processing these moments, so she is able to lay them to rest as they are-with peace.

We can say all throughout our pregnancies, "I'm just going with the flow, or we'll see what happens"; and act as though we aren't entering our births with expectation. But really that feels quite impossible with the many resources, information and opinions that are in our faces and at our fingertips. We begin our births with stories that we've surrounded ourselves with, our own past experiences and snippets of others. When we meditate or sit with the thought of, or make little preparations and set loving intention for the upcoming birth-we are fine lining expectation. It becomes nearly unavoidable, really.

So why are women made to feel that they need to silence their disappointment or feelings of trauma that may surround their birth story?

So many of us leave our stories untold, almost trying to erase pages rather than honoring and understanding them. When this happens, feelings of loneliness, regret, disappointment, sadness, anger, guilt, confusion etc... begin to sink deep. A woman's trauma after birth doesn't just disappear if she/we ignores it or it is met with invalidation. Many women that are still carrying hurt, will smile as she is silencing her screams. Feeling a prisoner to her own emotions. They lodge themselves within our womb space, which is very much connected to our heart space.

Severing the two in attempt for one to lead over the other doesn't or perhaps better put, cannot create the environment necessary for our growth and personal expansion. If we are to visualize these two as one, there really is no better picture than of a flower. Our womb space as the roots that both extends and continues into the earth and then also connects through an energetic stem that unravels upwardly into our bulb of a heart space. The more we tend to our roots, and establish a healthy foundation made of nurture and love- through positive thought and connection to our wombs, the stronger and more illuminated our blooming hearts can become. Our heart space is our connective point between our higher self and our earthly being. Our heart space is how we connect to others, how we follow through in trust, show compassion and gift forgiveness *(to ourselves and others)*. Our womb space or sacral holds our emotions, creativity, sexuality, and confidence. It's how we put into play our hearts desire to love and radiate joy. If our womb space and heart space become disconnected, just as a flower is plucked, it will only take so long before it begins to wilt and dry. Leaving the roots in a state of dormancy, so to speak. Our hearts begin to tire and close. This causes us to forget just how deserving we are to feel our inner beauty and love for ourselves. Which in turn makes it so much more difficult to pour that into other areas, whether that be our partner, children, career, art, or *healing*.

This severing or silencing can leave us feeling a sense of dis-alignment within ourselves. We may find ourselves feeling unworthy, unable, or even broken.

Each time we story share with another that can fully hold witness to our expression, there is a switching on of gears in our physical body and its stress responses. Stress hormones like cortisol, which can play a role in strengthening our traumatic memory, and epinephrine are reduced. Then hormone responses that actually encourage healing like oxytocin, dopamine, and endorphins surge.

The nervous system begins to soften and relax, helping the mama to fall into a restful state a bit easier, her appetite enhances, her mood balances, and her sleep improves. These are all things that help in our healing. Yes?...

Story sharing truly is potent medicine.

love

Notes

Feel Freely.

Honor where you are in your healing. Remind

yourself often that your feelings are valid and

deserving of your attention. When women are met

with even unintentional resistance and told to let go

of the uncomfortable, in ways and words similar to,

"at least your baby is healthy", "it could have been

worse" or, "it's over now" ...her feelings don't just

dissipate into thin air. Her feelings begin to dig

inward and downward deep. These heavier

emotions are left wandering about and become the

wounds that are later easily triggered. Give yourself

permission to freely acknowledge the happenings that

hurt you. By releasing our "negative" emotions we

are in a sense taking ownership of them and in turn,

taking a more manageable approach to the healing

from them.

A birth labyrinth is a meditative tool and is symbolic to the transformation that takes place as a woman moves into motherhood. A mindful expression in how there is only one entrance and one exit. Postpartum healing is very much the same. The story has already been laid in time. It has happened and we cannot change it. So, the only way to heal from the areas that pang, is to learn how to navigate through them as is.

A mother moving through her experience and saying, "this is what happened to me and this is how it makes me feel" is an incredibly important and powerful tool in the path to healing. This time of healing is yours. It doesn't require a stamp of approval or have to look one specific way.

The following labyrinth can be used to trace over with your index finger. As you move towards the center, think about the days leading up to your birth. Perhaps you feel the weather on your skin, hear the voices that loved on you, the rolls in your womb space, or the excitement and eagerness you felt to meet your baby.

As you near the center allow your thoughts to sit with your laboring self and then the birth of your baby.

While moving away from the center think about your first few weeks or month of your new experience as a mother, even if this wasn't your first birth.

As you trace over the labyrinth take note of any emotions that bubble up for you.

When you feel exquisite joy or pride, or a memory that cracks a smile, pause and sit with that memory for a bit. Appreciate this moment.

When you feel sadness or regret- whatever the sticky emotion it may be, again, pause and allow yourself to feel this fully. Allow your feelings to expand around this memory rather than interrupt it, push it aside or ignore it. Allow yourself to hold space for this memory and the feelings that come up from it. Then add an affirmation to this memory before continuing.

If you find yourself continually needing to pause at the same memory each time you sit with your labyrinth, that's ok! The goal of each of these practices is to feel our way back to peace within our hearts and within our thoughts. To reclaim our healing and our sovereignty. To create safe space to break things down, to rebuild, and to hold ourselves wholly as we grow and transform. The goal is to comfortably return home within ourselves, and this takes time.

Examples of Affirmations

My feelings are worthy

I forgive

I am working to release all pain

I am safe

I am free

I allow emotions to flow freely through me

I honor where I am in my healing journey

I am not broken. I am whole.

I am love and love is me.

I choose to leave a legacy of love

Your own affirmations

Another lovely practice is creating your own clay labyrinth. If you'd like, cut this page out or find a picture of a labyrinth and print it out. You can than purchase modeling clay and lay the print over the rolled-out clay and trace the labyrinth with your finger to leave an impression. Once dry, the new labyrinth can be decorated and sealed. A beautiful way to further symbolize the uniqueness of our births.

Thoughts...

Forgiveness.

First, forgive yourself. Whatever guilt or blame, anger or sadness... etc. that you may be carrying, it is important that the point of this processing is to let it go. To free ourselves from the experience. This isn't to say that we should disregard the current state of emotion, but rather aim to find a balance between honoring these feelings and working through them and then letting them go. Forgive yourself, then....

Forgive

Forgive

Forgive

And forgive again. For the sake of your own damn peace! Just like with any recovery after trauma or dealing with any essence of grief-things may need to be sat with more than once. They may need to be sat with over and over again. That's ok! As we've heard so often before-healing is not linear. Healing is individual and personal.

I love you

I'm sorry

Please forgive me

Thank you

I'd like to share with you now, the Ho'oponono Mantra. A Hawaiian prayer of forgiveness. I hope it leads your higher heart to harmony as well.

Ho'oponono is a peaceful yet powerful practice that I feel gifts clarity and assists in the untangling of many knotted emotions that can come with processing a birth.

Incorporating this into my day helped so much in releasing any of the resentment, anger, guilt or shame I was holding on to. Whether it was towards myself or the other individuals that played a role in the emotional wounds that surround my birth experience.

There are many ways to practice Ho'oponono. Books that offer guidance and information, as well as beautifully guided mediations available on YouTube and such. In my own practice, I sit comfortably and allow myself to move from any hustling thoughts and fall into my heart center. I breathe deep into this space for a few breaths.

Once I feel ready, I repeat the mantra for however long feels good. Often times I even feel pulled to move through this practice while driving and will speak the words for the length of a stop light.

When I first began using the Ho'oponono mantra I found myself having a difficult time connecting. My mind often falling into, "What am I even asking forgiveness for?" I hadn't done anything. I was the one that was hurting because of this, that, or, them. One afternoon while sitting with one specific moment of my birth, a blanket of realization came over me. The magic isn't in forgetting the wrongdoings or discomfort-but rather the peaceful opportunity to step into the power of choice. To take charge of the moving forward motion and to recognize this power is within-not the person or the situation. To understand that it is us that molds and rebuilds into our next. To be able to release ourselves from emotional shackles, to step into and through our healing, we have to learn how to call it our own.

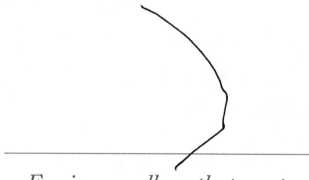

Forgiveness allows the peace to

settle in and get comfortable.

Factor in Your Truth.

Take moments to sit with the parts of your

story that went well, along with the

moments that didn't. The point of practicing

birth story healing isn't to dig something up

that isn't there, or to search for what went

unplanned. Unplanned is birth. The

unexpected should be the only thing that is

expected, because birth really does do its own

thing, every single time.

But…

It is ok, even healthy, to feel through any "negative" emotions that may be surrounding your birth experience. It's the ignoring that can send a mother spiraling. Where emotions can begin to affect our motherhood and relationship to self and others. Holding onto and shoving aside our feelings can cause a leaking over into other areas very soon after birth. Affecting breastfeeding, bonding with baby, physical healing, and the relationship with the partner.

In the following writing practice is space to begin listing both the areas of your birth that feel really good to sit with, as well as the moments that don't. After you have created your lists, take a look at the- "things I didn't love about my birth" list. Next to each, write one or two descriptive words that first come to mind that surround this memory.

Example:

"During my birth, early into my active labor and as contractions began to intensify, I expressed my desire to move into the bathtub. One of midwives told me no simply because she felt like things would move faster if I remained where I was-the birth stool.

As my labor progressed I shared my intense need to lay down and rest as I was beginning to fall asleep between each wave. In return I was met with more resistance and was told I need to remain on the stool or think about the hospital."

This made me feel <u>unsupported</u> and <u>disrespected.</u>

After you have given each memory a feeling. Take time to reflect on each. Without rushing, and as you process each, start to match the heavy emotion/feeling with a lesson or reminder that in turn you are (or practicing moving towards) thankful for or feel newly inspired by.

Example:

This memory has reminded me that my feelings, opinions, and needs are valid. I can speak up for myself in situations that may cause discomfort. I am thankful for the reminder that I do not need permission to step into my inner power and can speak my needs.

Now when one of your listed memories comes to mind, you will have these as a gentle reminder in how to switch gears within the thought. Again, as the particular situation comes to thought, hold it and allow it space to be exactly as it is. Then repeat your written words to yourself until you fall back into a more peaceful state.

Things I really loved about my

birth

Things I didn't love about my birth

"You don't have to turn this into something. It doesn't have to upset you."- Marcus Aurelius.

I sat with this quote for some time after my seventh birth. I had screenshot it to my phone because when I read it, it at first rang true. During the rawness of the early postpartum days I found myself wondering then, what was I supposed to do with all these feelings? Was I turning nothing into something?

I didn't want to feel upset. I wanted to look at my baby and only sit with the gratitude and the intense love that I have for her. I wanted to reflect on our birth story and smile rather than cry. But if I were to remain in a state of honesty with myself, I felt traumatized.

HOW DO I EXPLAIN
THIS FEELING?

Acknowledging these emotions isn't creating your pain, it's already very much there. If you have decided to work through this book, I'm sure you don't need anyone to tell you this. You feel it every day!

Acknowledging and honoring these emotions is the power a mother can use to harness and reclaim. To simply break chains of the repetitive, "what if's", guilt, blame, disappointment that she may be feeling; so her heavy feelings regarding her birth journey can surface, be seen, and eventually be released.

Call it what it is....

Thoughts....

Forgo the Silence.

Break away from this cycling of silence that we so often feel pulled to hold together. Even more so after birth, when we are programmed to think the only emotion we should be expressing is gratitude.

Speak from your heart space, not so much your head space–don't be your brains bitch, be your hearts hero. Hold space for yourself to spill! Allow the space to pour over and hear what your heart has to say, teach, expand, and heal you. Our emotional state begins to heal when we feel heard and validated– this begins within ourselves.

Wherever or however your birth happened, taking back power in how our feelings surround the birth is a first step in putting down the burden of ache we may be feeling after birth.

When I first began using the term "traumatized" to describe my feelings it felt a bit melodramatic, playing the victim or just over done. Was I feeling sorry for myself? Was I wallowing in the unraveling and not leaning enough into gratitude? However, that is very much what I felt when my processing began and still where I am in my healing writing this today.

Birth trauma is so much more than what outwardly transpired during the experience, or what may have been seen and felt from the outside looking in. This is about the unfolding and inner perception of the Mother and how she feels about it afterward.

As many as 1 in 3 women feel that their birth was traumatizing, complicated, or disappointing. A 2010 study by Alcorn also found that 46% of the 933 women shared that their birth experiences fell under a blanket definition of traumatic.

Describing our story as traumatic only feels incorrect if we are comparing! Today we tend to have an unintentional but habitual reaction of competitiveness and comparison around our births and birth stories—which has no room for such limiting views and approaches.

Traumatic is literally defined as emotionally

 disturbing

distressing

heartbreaking

Stressful....

A traumatic birth doesn't have to be physical injury or pain, although unfortunately often is. It doesn't have to mean an operating room, intervention, or particular setting. These can all just become ingredients to what the mother is actually aching from. In fact, a 2017 study found that Mothers that consider their birth journey to have been traumatic are actually speaking from an experience that surrounds lack of control rather than severe physical pain.

Source:

www.ncbi.nlm.nih.gov/pmc/articles/PMC5509770/

I can personally attest to this in reflection of several of my own birth experiences. My fifth babe spent her first week and half in the NICU. Seeing our tiny baby intubated and unable to touch and hold her was painful beyond words. Although this felt at the time to be the most difficult experience I had yet been pushed to evolve through, I never felt the pain and heaviness I carried after my seventh birth. The difference? The support, respect, trust, and love that I was surrounded by during the unfolding and afterwards. Traumatic is an appropriate definition.

You don't need permission from your mother, partner, midwife, sister, best friend, doctor, or neighbor in feeling your way through this. You are absolutely able to feel a great amount of gratitude and love while feeling disappointment, regret, and sadness. We don't lose our humanness when our children are born into this world. Our birth experiences are so much more than "At least she… has a healthy baby, got to have the homebirth that she wanted, didn't have a cesarean, she can do it again, or that it is over now." So forth and so on...All of these responses and similar that are made to a mother expressing her pain literally make me cringe.

Speaking your story freely, fully and feeling supported without judgement helps us to build new meaning and understanding. Sharing and feeling freely gifts the mother clarity and healing.

Your pain isn't breaking you. Its watering your strength and sprouting your wisdom. It's the beginnings of a new blossoming. Remain soft and trust the growing pains. You are so loved.

Mindful practices that encourage us to step outside of the silence and begin piecing the story back together.

- *Write it out. Without any other reason than just to spill.*

- *Get your records. This can offer insight and offer answers to the blurred areas of your birth experience.*

- *Write a letter to the people that hurt you. Even if you have no intention of sending, the release itself is powerful. Burning the letter(s) safely can also be beautifully symbolic of the release. Fire holds the energy of wisdom, purification and is invoking; encouraging the release of heavy attachment to the traumatic experience.*

- *Share your story with people that you feel safe with.*

- *Sit with the Earth and allow yourself to melt into her. When we are working through big feeling experiences our emotions and our feelings can become fueled and wrongly aimed. Grounding ourselves offers these feelings somewhere to land. As the earth holds space for us our internal rhythms fall back into balance.*

- *Practice breath work and meditation, such as yoga nidra.*See mama made shout out page.*

- *Record your story aloud. Sometimes hearing our stories in reflection can offer new perspective.*

Face your Triggers.

A trigger is anything that causes an emotional response in a way that it propels us back into the trauma due to cellular attachment. This relapsing can cause us to feel bombarded with the same behaviors that we may have experienced early on or before we took charge of our healing. This resurfacing can be subconscious or situational. Either or, if we don't learn to face the triggers– how to consciously apply a healthy amount of detachment from these triggers, we can quickly become prisoner to our traumatic experience. Triggers aren't completely negative, however. They offer us a little window to be able to peer into the areas that still need our attention and time. A reminder to lean into our healing.

If you were to flip roles for a moment and imagine that you were holding space for another mother carrying a similar experience and feeling traumatized and lost in her story unfolding; what would you say to her? Would you speak the same words to her as you do yourself?

In this practice I'd like you to begin by writing, honestly, the words you silently speak to yourself when your story replays in your thoughts.

Now, after taking a few moments to sit with what has been written, rewrite your responses as if you were relaying them to a mother at the park or to a close friend. Notice how you would wrap your heart around theirs and speak kindly and encouraging to her. Remind yourself that you are also deserving of these same words of wisdom. Your words of love!

This can become a useful tool when you feel yourself triggered and can help to create the healing space of reflection necessary to continue on your brave journey to peaceful power.

Words to self

In the space of reflection,

acceptance and peace is possible

Final thoughts

There are times when an experience leaves us feeling uncomfortable, vulnerable, confused, or traumatized etc... that we can end up picking it to pieces. We expand each moment within the experience until it's so stretched thin and pixelated that none of the pieces fit together anymore or make any sense. Sparking even more question, confusion, and heavy heartedness. Its important that we take the moments we find ourselves sitting with often and bring them back down in size again. To something more manageable to wrap our heads and hearts around. We then can begin to notice that it isn't that our answers or reasons aren't there, we are just looking for something that perhaps feels a bit better placed. If we pause and allow ourselves to cease the search and hold the moments as they are, the moment can then become easier to comprehend. More comfortable to accept as is, and our hearts move into a space to just let be. From here the healing begins.

The expression of trauma, holding space for our

stories, and honoring the internal narrative of the

experience carries such a delicate balance between

feeling our way through and allowing it to become

an anchor. The intention isn't to sit in a space of

processing forever, the intention is the commitment

to the rising from and the propelling forwardness

into alignment with our recent rebirth as Mama.

The intention is to step into accountability and the

power over how we choose to dance into our next.

The intent of awareness around our trauma should

never feel self-sabotaging, it should feel as if weight

is lifting and we are breathing in deep and full

again.

Favorite plant allies that may help alleviate postpartum discomforts like baby blues, fatigue, anxiety, insomnia, and depression.

Although I have leaned into each of these plant medicines and feel comfortable in their assistance during my own postpartum and beyond, please take these recommendations as if I were sharing simply as a friend. This is in no way shared as medical advice. The following list offers just a toes dip into the many benefits of each. I encourage the reader to dive into the opportunity to expand personal knowledge about the healing benefits and interaction of each plant friend.

Tulsi- Stress relief, hormone balancing (cortisol), and strengthens the nervous system.

Motherwort-Calms anxiety, helps insomnia, heart palpitations, uterine tonic, heart healing. *Motherwort wraps her energy around us like a true mama bear. She is ready to stand up against nearly anything we need to lean into her for. Her spirit offers guidance and encourages trust.*

Ashwagandha-Reduces both anxiety and depression symptoms, as well as general irritability on those tougher days, supports adrenal function, immune boosting, helps sleep, while gently increasing energy.

Lemon Balm and Catnip-Melancholy medicine, encourages calmness, decreases feelings of agitation.

Often times catnip spirit is said to connect us to our animalistic tendencies but her medicine speaks to me with much more depth. Nepeta Cataria was a first plant ally I felt truly connected to and experience with plant spirit healing medicine. Catnip is feminine and delicately sweetly scented, yet laced with bitterness. Her leaves and blooms calming, while her roots stimulating. She carries the energy of the sun and moon, along with the element of water. For me and what her spirits offers the most is a call for balance.

Shatavari-Hormone balancing, natural immune boosting, encourages milk production, gifts calming and grounding energy, cleansing and supportive to the reproductive system.

Oat straw-Nourishes the nervous system, helps restore vital minerals like calcium and magnesium, offers balance within the adrenal glands, tends to brain fog (mom brain).

Clary Sage-Gifts relief from baby blues, depression, anxiety, fatigue and insomnia. Regulates bowl movements, offers hormonal support, lifts mood, moon time (your period) support and relief.

Clary sage spirit teaches and reminds us that our feelings and emotions are valid, inspires harmony, and encourages us to do the inner work necessary in overcoming difficulty, specially within our hearts.

Gota Kola- Beneficial to the nervous system helping relieve fatigue, promotes metal clarity, and a wonderful tonic for the connective tissue while uterine ligament tone is returning. I love to pair this with Ashwagandha. I also infuse homemade ghee with gota kola and Moringa.

Nettles-A beautiful full body tonic and blood builder. Helps treat weakness due to anemia and calming in times of stress.

Nettles spirit offers us the message to stay open to receive while maintaining healthy boundaries. To remain in mindful flow of movement to avoid stagnancy.

Skullcap- Relieves postpartum blues by reducing tension, supporting the nerves, and encouraging rest if the mama has become overstimulated or over exhausted.

Skullcap spirit is similar to Motherwort, but more like the favorite Aunt than Mama bear.

cbd- Assists the mothers mind by relieving anxiety, depression and stress. In the physical body it helps in pain relief, immune response, and heart health.

Mama Mixes

<u>Postpartum hair loss and scalp mask</u> -

In a jar bring together a spoonful of activated charcoal, with coconut oil and avocado oil. Hemp oil is another really great option. Mix until it becomes an easy to spread paste. Add in a capsule of Biotin and a few drops of tea tree, rosemary and carrot seed oil. One or all is fine. I also like to infuse oil with rosemary, comfrey, lavender, clary sage, pine, fenugreek, nettle, and rose to use as the base of this mix. Adding in honey, baking soda, or even aloe are some other great options. Feel inspired to play around with it. Massage the paste into your scalp. Turning focus to the ends of your hair, esp if long, use castor oil or Aragon oil. Twist into a bun and go about your business until ready to wash out. I often do this in the evening and wash out the next morning. This mix helps to gently exfoliate and cleanse the scalp while stimulating new hair growth.

<u>Womb warming skin tightening massage paste</u> -

Combine a tsp of turmeric, cinnamon, clover, ginger, cardamom-any warming spices. Slowly mix in oil of choice, like coconut or sesame oil until you have a thick paste. When ready to use, take about a tsp of the mix and begin gently and lovingly massaging into your womb space and abdomen. The partnering of the spices and massage generates warmth and increases blood flow. This can help alleviate discomfort during menstruation and aid in healing postpartum. Once rubbed into skin, you can wrap the abdomen with a belly band or Bengkung belly wrap. Keep paste on for a few hours at least, beginning 7-10 days after a vaginal birth and after incision is healed, around 6 weeks, with caesarean birth. This will temporarily stain the skin. Avoiding contact with clothing is recommended. This paste can be used as often as you'd like. I also enjoy adding frankincense, clary sage, or lavender oil as well.

<u>Boob to bum balm</u> - 8oz mango butter and up to 1 oz bees wax. A tbsp of chamomile, lavender, yarrow, comfrey, nettles and fennel. Or you can use a tea bag of several of these

options if there is difficulty finding these herbs. (mountianroseherbs.com and Amazon are great resources)

With slow and *low heat, simmer the herbs in the butter for at least 30 mins, longer the better but be mindful not to burn. Slowly melt in bees wax. The amount used depends on the consistency you prefer.(If you'd like the balm to be a softer more creamer consistency use a little less wax). Remove from heat and as the balm cools, add a dropper full of rose hip oil and calendula oil. Strain into jar and cool completely. Feel free to add essential oils if you'd like. I often add fennel oil, frankincense, or melaleuca. This balm has been my go-to for years. I use it on baby's bottom, dry skin, sore nipples, and even to boost milk supply or heal clogged duct/mastitis, by massaging into the breast and armpit area and then sitting with warm compress between feedings. The left over herbs or tea bag can be frozen and used for bumps and scraps.

Milky Mama Biscuits -

1c GF or regular all-purpose flour

1c oat flour

1/3c maple syrup

1/2c butter or earth balance

1/2c coconut butter or can just increase regular butter but coconut butter is rich in lauric acid which can help boost the immune system and milk supply. Lauric acid can also relieve morning sickness symptoms. Ghee is another delicious alternative.

2tbsp goji berries

4-5 large dates and or apricots

1.5tsp hemp seed

1/3c black sesame seed

1.5 tsp Shatavari

Tea of choice. I use nettles, lemon balm, chamomile, moringa, red raspberry etc...

Preheat oven to 350*. Begin by brewing tea of choice, we'll use nettles as the example. Along with the tea, steep the goji berries, apricots, and dates in the nettle tea. In the meantime, combine flours, butters, maple syrup, sesame seeds, and Shatavari. Add the fruit into the mix and then slowly 1-2 tbsp of tea. Once well mixed, refrigerate covered for at least 30 mins.

After the dough has cooled, dust counter space with organic powdered sugar and roll dough into a thin 3-5cm sheet. Using the top of a mason jar cut cookies and transfer to lined baking sheet. Bake for 10-15 min or once edges just begin to brown. Allow to cool *completely.

Tuck in Stew

 1 head of cauliflower

2tbsp curry powder

1-2 cloves of garlic chopped

Paprika, cumin, fennel seed, turmeric and fenugreek, and salt/pepper (Frontier co-op brand has a curry powder that is combined with both the turmeric and fenugreek-its YUM!)

Olive oil

¼ red onion chopped

Kale, carrots, squash. Really any veggie that you enjoy

1c plant-based milk

55

Optional mix ins- Astragalus and Reishi (Superfeast is an excellent company to purchase from)

Wash and cut the cauliflower into manageable chunks. Season with curry powder and ½-1 tsp of the rest of the spices and drizzle with olive oil. Enough to coat and beautifully color each piece of cauliflower. Roast until tender.

Once cooked, add the cauliflower to a blender or chop into a rice like consistency. Add to a stock pot or similar, heat a little more oil and begin to cook your veggies w a little salt and pepper. Once the mix is aromatic and beginning to soften, add 4c of veggie broth or bone broth and stir in the cauliflower. Allow to simmer together on low heat until the veggies are fully cooked through and soft. Slowly add in the plant-based milk and stir. Delicious topped with Go Raw tangy coconut chips.

If cauliflower or even the kale is too much for digestion, and often can be in the early postpartum days, it is easily replaced with a well-cooked brown rice or quinoa.

Your Birth Story

ABOUT THE AUTHOR

Passionate and determined about her own journey to regain self-assertiveness, sovereignty, and healing after her seventh birth; one that left her feeling deeply disrespected, silenced, and abandoned, Arianna began building and seeking tools to assist in finding her way back to self. With time and in the creation of this project, birth story debriefing, and connecting to many inspiring women; she regained her voice, found new truth, and continues to move towards accepting her birth story with peace.

Alongside Mothering her seven children Arianna has been working with women during their own pregnancy and birth journeys since pregnant with her second babe, in 2005. Arianna created a childbirth education class specially designed to uplift, encourage, and support teen mothers as she felt this was something lacking during her own teen pregnancy experience. Through these connections she began branching off and supporting woman and their families through full spectrum Doula work. In 2009 she stepped away from birth work completely, to turn full attention to her family while they moved from Colorado to Texas, where she still lives today. Arianna has now begun moving back into connecting with other mothers through conscience conception guidance, birth story debriefing, sacred space and birth preparation and postpartum support. With her babes in tow, she marvels in the magic of plant spirit healing, embodied movement medicine, art, and a big bowl of ice cream. To connect, Arianna can be reached through email at encompassingherdivinity@gmail.com . For updates on gatherings and offerings she can be found on Instagram at oh_thathippiemomwlotsofkids. #IlluminatingHerStory

Made in the USA
Lexington, KY
24 February 2019